CHILD WELFARE LEAGUE OF AMERICA

Guidelines for the Development of Foster Care Handbooks

What Foster Youth Have to Say

Terry Harrak, Project Coordinator
Maria Garin Jones, MSW, Project Manager

CWLA Press • Washington, DC

CWLA Press is an imprint of the Child Welfare League of America. The Child Welfare League of America is the nation's oldest and largest membership-based child welfare organization. We are committed to engaging people everywhere in promoting the well-being of children, youth, and their families, and protecting every child from harm.

CHILD WELFARE LEAGUE OF AMERICA, INC.
440 First Street, NW, Third Floor
Washington, DC 20001-2085
E-mail: books@cwla.org

CURRENT PRINTING (last digit)
10 9 8 7 6 5 4 3 2

Cover design by Tung Mullen
Text design and editing by Kristen Kreisher

Printed in the United States of America

ISBN # 0-87868-812-9

Contents

Acknowledgments

This project was made possible through the generous support of the Annie E. Casey Foundation.

The Youth Involvement Initiative would also like to express its gratitude to its youth consultants: Amy Clay, Jenny Velazquez, and Walika Cox.

Introduction

Entry into the foster care system is often a difficult transition for children, and it can be an even more confusing and frightening time when they are not provided with the information needed to understand the system. To bridge this information gap and ease the transitions in and out of care, the Youth Involvement Initiative, working in conjunction with the National Foster Care Awareness Project, brought together youth currently and formerly in foster care to discuss the use and improvement of foster care handbooks.

This group of youth, acting as project consultants, concluded that providing a well-crafted handbook to every youth in foster care would be a positive first step and drafted some basic standards for agencies seeking to create resources for youth in foster care. These guidelines include a list of key questions that should be addressed, critical subject areas to be covered, and an outline of the components of an effective handbook.

Although a foster care handbook can be a valuable resource to a child in care, it should never be used as a substitute for adult support. The youth who participated in this initiative stressed the need for every young person in foster care to have the ongoing support of a caring adult who is willing to invest in a quality relationship. Developing this invaluable relationship requires spending time with the young person and getting to know him or her well—asking questions and listening to goals, fears, hopes, and dreams.

This overview of foster care handbooks can serve as a starting point for agencies interested in providing an informative handbook that can help to promote successful transitions for all foster youth.

The Process

For the first phase of the assessment, the consultants were brought together and asked to brainstorm on the following questions:

Think about your experiences in foster care:
What did you need to know?
What were some of the questions you needed answered?

This session, originally scheduled for 30 minutes, became a two-hour discussion. The consultants had much to share about the lack of information and support they received during their first days in the foster care system. One young woman, recently reunited with her maternal grandmother in a kinship placement after four years in foster care, is still uncertain about why she and her siblings were removed from their home. She emphasized that knowing why you have been placed in foster care is an integral part of the interaction that needs to occur at the onset of a child's placement. Clearly, youth should receive this information from adults involved with them. Resources such as foster care handbooks, however, should reinforce the information.

Formulating Key Questions

Amidst the stress and confusion that are associated with placement in foster care, young people often give little thought to the questions they want to ask their social workers. Initially, the consultants worked on the development of frequently asked questions for foster care youth. It soon became apparent, however, that the answers to some questions would vary from state to state. As a result, the consultants opted to develop a list of *key questions* that should be addressed when developing state foster care handbooks. The list addresses a variety of placement and transitional issues, including general information, financial preparation, networks of support, educational opportunities, health care, housing, and employment options (see Appendix A). This list is intended to identify pertinent issues as attempts are made to develop handbooks tailored to specific state policies and procedures.

Designating Critical Subject Areas

To assess existing state handbooks for their strengths and weaknesses and formulate suggested standards, the consultants reviewed five state foster care handbooks. Although many states have developed handbooks for youth in foster care, the Youth Involvement Initiative decided, for the purposes of this initiative, to limit the review to five states. The state handbooks selected came from Maine, Kentucky, Mississippi, Tennessee, and Florida.

After assessing the strengths and weaknesses of each handbook, the consultants identified the *critical subject areas* they felt were the most important, including:

- Contents
- Introduction
- Mission Statement
- Explanation of Foster Care
- Explanation of Why a Child Enters Foster Care
- Rights of Youth
- Responsibilities of Youth, Caseworkers, and Service Providers
- Grievance Process
- Resources
- Contacts
- Visitation
- Input from Youth
- Definition of Legal Terms
- Overview of Independent Living Services
- Questions to Ask
- How to Advocate for Yourself
- Foster Care Chain of Command
- Court Procedures and Legal Terminology
- Education
- Employment
- Housing
- Health Care
- Support
- Financial Preparation
- New Independent Living Legislation
- Transition Checklist
- Pertinent Information
- Graphics

The project team then developed a table comparing how well each state handbook addressed these areas (see Appendix B).

Outlining the Components of Effective Handbooks

The consultants also developed guidelines for effective handbooks by outlining *the eight components of effective handbooks* (see page 11).

Review of State Foster Care Handbooks

The consultants reviewed five state handbooks to determine how well each addressed the critical subject areas. The consultants especially stressed the importance of youth involvement and the need for appealing formatting and graphics when reviewing each state's book.

While each of the five handbooks provided valuable information and served a specific purpose for the state in which it was developed, this section provides a brief overview of each handbook's strengths and needs as assessed by the consultants. A complete comparative table is available in Appendix B.

Florida

The Florida handbook, *Foster Care through the Eyes of Teens,* is noteworthy for its bright blue color and compact size. Several of the consultants highlighted the fact that the handbook can "fit in your back pocket." The wording and graphics on the cover are also very appealing to youth. Perhaps the most interesting aspect of the handbook is the fact that the State Teen Advisory Board of Florida includes its mission statement on the first page of the handbook. This inclusion highlights the fact that young people can become involved in advocacy work within the state. It would be more helpful, however, if contact numbers were made available. Young people interested in becoming involved with the Advisory Board or needing additional information might be deterred by the absence of contact information.

Tennessee

The Tennessee *Handbook for Teens in State Custody* appears to be geared toward a younger population. The color of the print and the overall format of the handbook are appealing, but the graphics would be more effective if they corresponded better with the subject matter. It was helpful that the handbook provides an explanation of why a young person may be in foster care. Given the fact that the handbook was developed by the Tennessee Youth Advisory Council, it would be beneficial to include some quotes or inspirational vignettes written by these youth.

Kentucky

Kentucky's handbook, *Independent Living Guidebook for You*, is designed to address the needs and issues facing young people making the transition out of foster care, as opposed to entering the system. The handbook highlights a variety of issues, but does not provide comprehensive information to the reader. For example, one section highlights the Independent Living Teen Conference, but fails to include contact or follow-up information. The graphics are pleasing, but would be more so if they were in color. The consultants were concerned about the lack of introductory information in this handbook. For older adolescents who enter care and participate in the Independent Living services available in Kentucky, it would be helpful to have basic information about foster care, rights, and responsibilities. If there is another handbook that is distributed to foster youth, it might be beneficial to combine some of the information.

Mississippi

In Mississippi, the *Handbook for Teens in Foster Care* appears to be written by the Mississippi Department of Human Services, Division of Child and Family Services. The handbook notes, however, that several youth made contributions to its development. The handbook provides an excellent definition of foster care and makes a statement about why one child might be removed from their home, while siblings are able to remain. It also includes a Bill of Rights for Foster Children and is specific about the rights of children in care. The consultants reported, however, that the format was not well organized. Although the content was strong, a logical progression was not apparent for the information included in the text. A contents page would be helpful. Furthermore, the absence of graphics and use of black ink on white paper made the handbook a bit monotonous to read.

Maine

Answers...A Handbook for Youth by Youth in Foster Care was most favorably reviewed by the consultants. This handbook covers 22 of the 30 *critical subject areas* identified by the consultants. The cover graphics and the use of heavy cardstock indicated that a great deal of effort was put into the printing and publication of the document. The initial pages include contact information and instructions for using the handbook. The consultants also found the question and answer format to be helpful.

The Maine handbook is noteworthy for all of the extra features it includes. For example, the pocket folder in the back of the handbook is a nice touch, and the quotes from youth are a great addition. Young people need to be inspired and motivated by other youth who have had similar experiences. Throughout the handbook, the input and authorship of young people is evident. The chain of command section is interesting, but the consultants suggested that it would be helpful to include information—including names and phone numbers—on how to contact these personnel. The transition checklist is helpful, but the consultants suggested the handbook go beyond the checklist and supplement the existing information on transition issues. In general, the handbook is extremely comprehensive and user-friendly.

Eight Components of Effective Handbooks

The consultants suggested using the following format when designing a handbook for youth in foster care.

Part One: Introduction

This section should include:

1. Details on how the handbook could be used and who is responsible for its development.
2. A mission statement developed by the organization or group responsible for the handbook.
3. A contents page that provides a quick overview of the handbook's features.
4. An overview of foster care and a generic explanation for why a child is placed in care.

Part Two: Knowing Your Rights

An overview of rights should include:

1. The rights of youth, birth family, foster and adoptive parents, and care providers.
2. An overview of visitation policy and procedures, as well as implications for visitation with the youth's family.

3. The Bill of Rights for Foster Children.
4. An overview of responsibilities, including the responsibilities of youth, birth family, care providers, and foster and adoptive parents.
5. Information about the grievance procedure of the organization or agency that has custody of the young person, including names, addresses, and phone numbers for the personnel specific to the state. This section should assist young people who feel their rights have been violated and who wish to file a formal complaint.
6. Information about the chain of command so that youth have a sense of how the system is structured.
7. Information about how to advocate for oneself and a listing of advocacy resources, including the names, addresses, and telephone numbers of local, state, and national child advocacy organizations (see Appendix C).

Part Three: General Information

This section should provide:

1. An overview of confidentiality and what it means for youth in foster care.
2. Definitions of "system" and legal terminology.
3. An overview of placement options for youth in foster care.

4. An overview of independent living services for youth in foster care.
5. An overview of court procedures.

Part Four: Real Life Stories

To assure foster youth that they are not alone, this section should include:

1. A variety of inspirational quotes and anecdotes written by other young people in foster care.
2. An overview of opportunities for youth to become involved at the local, state, and national level. Contact information should be provided.

Part Five: Frequently Asked Questions

In developing a state-specific handbook, a group of foster youth should be asked to identify some questions that they had when they entered care. If this is not possible, consult Appendix A for a list of questions generated by youth currently and formerly in foster care.

Part Six: Independent Living Supplement

This section should offer guidance to a young person making the transition to adulthood. These youth face six major challenges: education, employment, housing, health care, financial preparedness, and support network. For each of the six challenges of transition, an overview of services specific to one's state should be provided. For example, in the education section, states should provide information regarding tuition waivers, funding to cover college applications and related expenses, and scholarships and stipends available to foster youth. The section should also include a transition checklist aimed at assisting foster youth with acquiring necessary documents and developing a timeline for obtaining insurance and employment might also be included.

Part Seven: The Foster Care Independence Act of 1999

This section should familiarize each youth with the John H. Chaffee Independence Program, established by the Foster Care Independence Act of 1999.

Part Eight: Personal Information and Notes

In this section, youth should have space to document important information, including the names, addresses, and phone numbers of family, friends, caregivers, and other members of his or her support network. Space for notes should also be included.

Summary

When the work of the consultants was initiated, they were asked to think about the type of information they needed as they entered foster care and when they made the transition from foster care to independence. The consultants identified a number of issues in the form of *key questions*. In reviewing the individual foster care handbooks from Maine, Mississippi, Tennessee, Florida, and Kentucky, the consultants initiated the process by highlighting the strengths and areas for improvement. As the review progressed, a number of *critical subject areas* emerged, eventually totaling 30 areas for consideration. From these critical subject areas, *eight components of effective foster care handbooks* were identified. The guidelines established in this document provide a template for the development of additional resources for foster youth.

Though the consultants were charged with the task of providing guidelines to those interested in designing handbooks that will be useful to youth in foster care, they also remained concerned about how the guidelines would be used in practice. The consultants emphasized that the distribution of foster care handbooks to youth does not address their need for the ongoing support of caring adults in their lives.

Throughout the process, the consultants underscored the fact that these are only guidelines to assist those interested in developing resources for youth in foster care. States interested in developing handbooks based on the guidelines provided should be aware that there is room for interpretation and the inclusion of other materials that could be helpful to youth.

To disseminate information about the challenges that young people transitioning out of foster care face, we need to reach out to all individuals involved in the lives of foster youth. Young people must be meaningfully engaged in the process because their stories and experiences are of paramount importance, and their voices should guide our efforts. The work of the Youth Involvement Initiative project team represents a starting point. It is intended to get people thinking, not only about what types of information young people in foster care need to have access to, but about the tremendous contributions that young people can make when they are provided with opportunities to be heard.

Appendix A: List of Key Questions

General Information

- How do I obtain my social security card?
- How do I obtain my birth certificate?
- Can I get a driver's license? If so, who will cover the costs for driver's education?
- How long will I have health insurance? Are there any programs that will assist me with health insurance once I am no longer covered by the state?
- How will I pay for medical visits and medications?
- Can I stay in foster care after my 18 birthday?
- Can I own a car?
- Do I have a role in determining my placement? Can I request a move to another placement?
- Can I participate in meetings, staffings, or conversations that pertain to me?
- Why am I in foster care?

- How and when will I see my birth family, siblings, etc.?
- Why do you have to go through all of my belongings?
- Do I have any privacy?
- Who can I call when I need to talk to someone or have a problem?
- What are the responsibilities of my foster parents and social workers?
- Do I have an attorney? If so, how do I contact him or her?

Financial Issues

- Can I manage the money I earn from a job?
- Can I open a bank account?
- Where can I get help with filing taxes?
- How can I establish a good credit history?
- Can I have a credit card? How many is too many?
- Who can I talk to about credit questions?
- How do I rent an apartment?
- Where can I get information about my credit history?

Support Network

- Who can I talk to when I need support?
- Can I call and see my family?
- What is the process for visiting my friends and family?
- Will the department help me and my family with transportation?
- Do I have access to community-based organizations such as the local YMCA, Big Brothers, Girl Scouts, and 4-H?
- Can I still go to my place of worship in my community of origin?
- Can I participate in afterschool and extracurricular activities with my friends?

Educational Issues

- Do I have to switch schools if I move?
- How do I access my educational records?
- Can I get a tutor if I need help with school?
- Can I go to college?
- Who will assist me with college applications?
- Can I visit the schools to which I apply?

- Is there financial assistance for college applications, SAT/ACT tests, and trips to visit schools?
- Is financial assistance available to me if I want to go to college?
- How do I pay for school activities, sports, pictures, prom, graduation, etc.?
- Can I get lunch money or do I have to eat "free lunch?"
- What support is available to me if I have a learning disability?
- Who is responsible for updating my IEP before I graduate from high school?

Health Issues

- What type of health insurance do I have?
- What do I do when I am sick?
- How do I get information on preventive medicine?
- How can I obtain information on health education, birth control, sexual behavior, and yearly checkups.

Housing Issues

- Do I have to share my living space or can I have my own room?

- Where will I live when I leave care?
- Are there any funds available to assist me with housing after I leave care?

Employment Issues

- Can I work while I'm in foster care?
- Will my independent living stipend be affected by how much I earn from my job?
- Will my earnings affect my foster care payments?
- Are there any job training programs available to me?
- How many hours can I work?
- Can I get assistance with transportation to work?

Appendix B: Critical Subject Areas

Component	State				
	ME	KY	MS	TN	FL
Contents	X	X			
Introduction	X		X		X
Mission Statement					X
Why I'm in Care? What is Foster Care?	X		X	X	
Rights of Youth	X		X[1]	X	X[2]
Responsibilities	X[3]			X[4]	X[5]
Grievance Process	X				
Resources					
Contacts	X				
Visitation	X		X	X	X
Quotes/Youth Voices	X				X
Definitions/Glossary	X				X
Overview of Independent Living Services	X	X	X	X	
Questions You Should Ask.	X	X			

Component	State				
	ME	KY	MS	TN	FL
How to Advocate for Yourself.					
Chain of Command	X				
Explanation of Confidentiality	X		X		
Court Procedures/ Legal Terminology	X	X	X		X
Education	X	X	X	X	X
Employment			X		
Housing			X		
Health Care	X		X		
Support			X		
Financial Preparation		X	X		
Ind. Living Legislation					
Transition Checklist	X	X			
Pertinent Information	X	X		X	
Written by Youth	X			X	X
Graphics	X				

Notes

1. Includes Bill of Rights for foster children
2. Includes rights of youth, foster/adoptive parents, and counselors
3. Includes biological family, provider, caseworkers.
4. Addresses youth responsibilities
5. Includes foster parents and counselors.

Appendix C: Sources of Additional Information

American Civil Liberties Union
125 Broad Street
New York, New York 1004-2110
WWW.ACLU.ORG

Children's Defense Fund
25 E Street NW
Washington, DC 20001
202/628 8787
WWW.CHILDRENSDEFENSE.ORG

Child Welfare League of America
440 First Street NW, Third Floor
Washington, DC 20001-2085
202/638-2952
WWW.CWLA.ORG

National Center for Youth Law
405 14th Street, 15th Floor
Oakland, California 94612
510/835-8098
WWW.YOUTHLAW.ORG

Youth Advocacy Center
281 6th Avenue
New York, New York 10014
212/675-6181
WWW.YOUTHADVOCACYCENTER.ORG

Youth Law Center
417 Montgomery Street, Suite 900
San Francisco, California 94104
415/543-3379
WWW.YOUTHLAWCENTER.COM

Youth Law Center - DC Office
Children's Legal Protection Center
1010 Vermont Avenue NW, Suite 310
Washington, DC 20005
202/637-0377

About the Authors

Terry Harrak

Ms. Harrak is a powerful advocate for young people involved with the foster care system. After two and one-half years in foster care, she found herself homeless shortly after her 18 birthday when she aged out of care. Despite seemingly insurmountable odds, Ms. Harrak has established herself as a strong voice for youth in care throughout the country. She is currently employed by the Youth Law Center and works with the Child Welfare League of America on the Youth Involvement Initiative. By the age of 20, she had testified before Congress, met with the First Lady and President Clinton, and attended the signing of the Foster Care Independence Act of 1999. Ms. Harrak is also working towards her college degree.

Maria Garin Jones, MSW

Ms. Garin Jones is currently the director of Youth Services at the Child Welfare League of America. She has worked with young people in a variety of settings to promote their successful transitions to adulthood. Ms. Garin Jones has an MSW from Virginia Commonwealth University. She earned her Bachelor's degree in education and psychology at Bucknell University.